Understanding PaaS

Michael P. McGrath

O'REILLY®

Beijing · Cambridge · Farnham · Köln · Sebastopol · Tokyo

Understanding PaaS
by Michael P. McGrath

Published by O'Reilly Media, Inc., 1005 Gravenstein Highway North, Sebastopol, CA 95472.

O'Reilly books may be purchased for educational, business, or sales promotional use. Online editions are also available for most titles (*http://my.safaribooksonline.com*). For more information, contact our corporate/institutional sales department: (800) 998-9938 or *corporate@oreilly.com*.

Editors:	Mike Loukides and Meghan Blanchette	**Cover Designer:**	Karen Montgomery
Production Editor:	Jasmine Perez	**Interior Designer:**	David Futato
Proofreader:	O'Reilly Production Services	**Illustrator:**	Robert Romano

Revision History for the First Edition:

    2012-01-12   First release

See *http://oreilly.com/catalog/errata.csp?isbn=9781449323424* for release details.

ISBN: 978-1-449-32342-4

[LSI]

1327420395

Table of Contents

Preface

For years, I worked as the Fedora Project's infrastructure team lead. It was quite possibly the best job I'll ever have. People were constantly coming up with new ideas and as the keeper of resources, they'd come to the infrastructure team to put those ideas into motion. Looking back, I have regret. It's about how many of those ideas I had to say no to just because there weren't enough people or servers to go around. So many projects just never got off the ground because of the high cost of innovation.

With all those never born projects in mind, I joined Red Hat's cloud computing initiative to make OpenShift a reality. OpenShift is Red Hat's Platform as a Service (PaaS) offering and it's the answer to so many problems I've had in the past, like those Fedora Project ideas that never got off the ground.

Yet, even months after OpenShift launched, I am constantly surprised how often people would ask me what PaaS is. Is it virtualization? Is it just cloud computing? Why would I use it? This book is the result of the questions so many people have asked me at conferences, on IRC, and via email. So to all of you curious and hardworking inventors out there, thank you. I hope the answers contained in this book will help you innovate even better.

Conventions Used in This Book

The following typographical conventions are used in this book:

Italic
> Indicates new terms, URLs, email addresses, filenames, and file extensions.

`Constant width`
> Used for program listings, as well as within paragraphs to refer to program elements such as variable or function names, databases, data types, environment variables, statements, and keywords.

`Constant width bold`
> Shows commands or other text that should be typed literally by the user.

Constant width italic

> Shows text that should be replaced with user-supplied values or by values determined by context.

 This icon signifies a tip, suggestion, or general note.

 This icon indicates a warning or caution.

Using Code Examples

This book is here to help you get your job done. In general, you may use the code in this book in your programs and documentation. You do not need to contact us for permission unless you're reproducing a significant portion of the code. For example, writing a program that uses several chunks of code from this book does not require permission. Selling or distributing a CD-ROM of examples from O'Reilly books does require permission. Answering a question by citing this book and quoting example code does not require permission. Incorporating a significant amount of example code from this book into your product's documentation does require permission.

We appreciate, but do not require, attribution. An attribution usually includes the title, author, publisher, and ISBN. For example: "*Understanding PaaS* by Michael P. McGrath (O'Reilly). Copyright 2012 Michael P. McGrath, 978-1-449-32342-4."

If you feel your use of code examples falls outside fair use or the permission given above, feel free to contact us at *permissions@oreilly.com*.

Safari® Books Online

 Safari Books Online is an on-demand digital library that lets you easily search over 7,500 technology and creative reference books and videos to find the answers you need quickly.

With a subscription, you can read any page and watch any video from our library online. Read books on your cell phone and mobile devices. Access new titles before they are available for print, and get exclusive access to manuscripts in development and post feedback for the authors. Copy and paste code samples, organize your favorites, download chapters, bookmark key sections, create notes, print out pages, and benefit from tons of other time-saving features.

O'Reilly Media has uploaded this book to the Safari Books Online service. To have full digital access to this book and others on similar topics from O'Reilly and other publishers, sign up for free at *http://my.safaribooksonline.com*.

How to Contact Us

Please address comments and questions concerning this book to the publisher:

O'Reilly Media, Inc.
1005 Gravenstein Highway North
Sebastopol, CA 95472
800-998-9938 (in the United States or Canada)
707-829-0515 (international or local)
707-829-0104 (fax)

We have a web page for this book, where we list errata, examples, and any additional information. You can access this page at:

http://shop.oreilly.com/product/0636920023128.do

To comment or ask technical questions about this book, send email to:

bookquestions@oreilly.com

For more information about our books, courses, conferences, and news, see our website at *http://www.oreilly.com*.

Find us on Facebook: *http://facebook.com/oreilly*

Follow us on Twitter: *http://twitter.com/oreillymedia*

Watch us on YouTube: *http://www.youtube.com/oreillymedia*

CHAPTER 1

What Is Cloud Computing?

Cloud computing is a funny business. The term itself is sometimes derided by technical professionals as meaningless. Yet, companies of all sizes, from the largest enterprises to small start-ups, are taking a serious look at it. Even the luddites are taking notice. So what is cloud computing? Why is it here? Perhaps most importantly, how much does it cost? These are all topics covered in this book. The focus is on how to utilize the cloud as a tool, not how to create and operate a private cloud.

At a high-level view, cloud computing provides a way for developers to focus exclusively on coding. It provides a way for systems engineers to finally offload some of the projects that have crept up over the years and continue to plague their time. With cloud technologies, architects can quickly prototype new technologies with minimum commitment and cost. These same technologies allow executives to better control and predict cost as well as remove much of the waste created by traditional computing. The differences between traditional computing and cloud computing are nuanced but many.

The rest of this chapter discusses the differences between the three primary cloud computing areas: Software as a Service (SaaS), Infrastructure as a Service (IaaS), and Platform as a Service (PaaS), pronounced "sass," "pass," and "i-a-a-s," respectively. Keep in mind that the field is new and changing. Rapid innovation of this kind causes the lines between IaaS, PaaS, and SaaS to blur, sometimes significantly. It won't always be obvious whether something is PaaS or IaaS but the difference between them isn't nearly as important as understanding the concepts of how to properly utilize these technologies.

Software as a Service (SaaS)

The idea of "Software as a Service" isn't new, but the term SaaS is. SaaS simply refers to software that is provided on-demand for use. Traditionally, when someone wanted to use software they'd go to the store, pick up some disks, take them home, and install them on a computer. With SaaS, they just use hosted software. There's no installation, no updates, no mess. There's no magic to it. Anyone who has used web mail of any kind has been using SaaS.

SaaS has really come into maturity over the last decade. Some modern SaaS providers do a lot of fancy work behind the scenes to make things function properly. Compare what engineers had to do to run web mail in the late 90s to what the team at Google does to run Gmail today.

If one of those web mail admins from the 90s were brought forward in time and told to use Gmail, they'd be impressed for sure, but the basic workflow and usage would be very familiar to them. If that same sysadmin was told to start running Gmail, he'd likely be completely lost. That's a common theme in cloud computing. Some aspects are so familiar, yet others are quite foreign when compared to traditional computing environments.

Infrastructure as a Service (IaaS)

Infrastructure as a Service (IaaS) isn't conceptually new. People have been collocating in data centers since data centers have been around. What is different with IaaS is the tooling behind it and where the lines of responsibility get drawn. Proper IaaS provides a mechanism for people to replace all of their data center hardware needs. Common IaaS services include:

- Host provisioning
- Load balancing
- Public and private network connectivity
- Firewalls
- Storage

Additionally, all of the dependencies for these services are also provided. This includes monitoring, power, cooling, repair, security, inventory tracking, and perhaps most importantly, people. Some IaaS providers even have convenient solutions to geographically diversify computing resources. All of this is provided at a cost that just isn't possible with traditional computing. Typical rates for a host are pennies an hour.

In practical terms, this means that the time between when someone decides they need to host to when they actually log into it has been greatly reduced to a couple of minutes. Developers don't have to put a large proposal together that includes servers, storage, network, rack space, installation, configuration, and so on. An entire proof of concept can be put together for the cost of a typical lunch. They don't have to wait hours for sysadmins to provision a host. They don't have to wait days for an order to get delivered and installed. Instead, with IaaS, they just need a little cash and a few minutes to pick what host they want.

Amazon Web Services (AWS)

The current front-runner for IaaS is Amazon Web Services (AWS), which is the brand Amazon.com has given to its cloud computing offerings. To give users an idea of the state of the art in IaaS, just look at AWS. The example below is a walk-through to create a new host via AWS's Elastic Compute Cloud (EC2), which is the most common way users of AWS create hosts. This host is a virtual machine created on-demand with the parameters set via a wizard. Without getting too deep into IaaS, it is important to understand these core concepts, as almost all of cloud computing is based on an underlying IaaS layer.

This example illustrates the steps to create a new host. First, log in to *https://aws.amazon.com/* (we're assuming here an account has already been created).

Next, select the EC2 tab. This tab brings up the display showin in Figure 1-1.

The Launch button shown in Figure 1-1 starts the wizard to provision a new host. Notice in the lefthand navigation bar that there is a drop-down option for Region; in this example, US East (Virginia) is selected. This means the work done during this example will be in this region. Building hosts in Ireland or Tokyo is as simple as changing the drop-down.

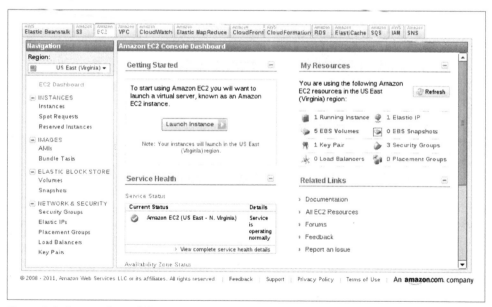

Figure 1-1. Amazon Launch Page

As shown in Figure 1-2, select a Red Hat Enterprise Linux image called an Amazon Machine Image or AMI. In its simplest terms, an AMI is a set of default configurations for a virtual machine as well as the underlying operating system. An AMI is somewhat analogous to a physical machine that is powered off.

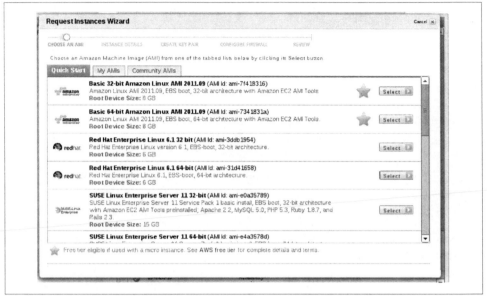

Figure 1-2. AWS RHEL Selection

Next, select the virtual machine's details, as shown in Figure 1-3. Notice the bullet in the wizard refers to this as an "instance detail." AWS refers to virtual machines as instances. Pick a micro instance for this demo.

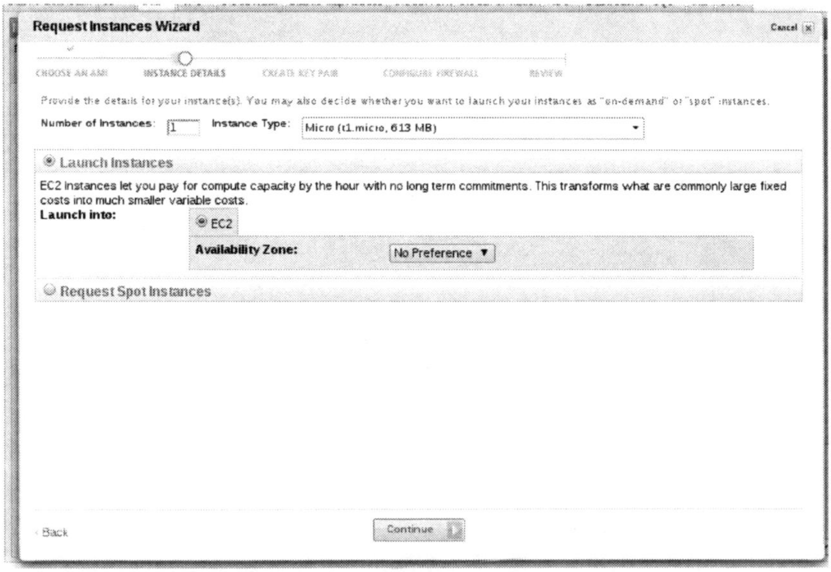

Figure 1-3. Instance Details

The screen shown in Figure 1-4 allows users to create key and value pairs called tags. A default key called "name" is provided to identify the instance. By default these tags have no impact on the actual running host. They're typically used to provide an easier way to track and manage AWS resources. Common tags might include owner, environment, and so on. This instance is called Demo1.

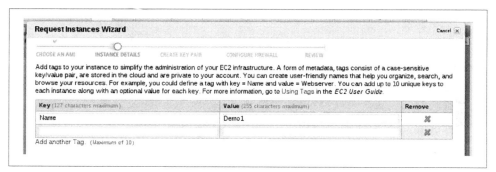

Figure 1-4. Instance Details Key Value

The screen shown in Figure 1-5 is important, and is different then the key tags mentioned in the previous screen shot. The key selected in this portion is the private SSH key used to authenticate with the virtual machine. If a new key is created, this is the step in which it would be downloaded. These are SSH public/private key pairs and it is considered best practice in AWS to use them to access a newly created instance.

Figure 1-5. Create Key Pair

 Once booted, users can choose whatever authentication mechanisms they want. The key simply gets downloaded from a special AWS website (From an instance it's *http://169.254.169.254/latest/meta-data/public-keys/0/openssh-key*) and then placed in /root/.ssh/authorized_keys. There are lots of handy tricks available at that site for customization of newly booted instances. See the EC2 User Guide and forums for more information.

Figure 1-6 shows the Configure Firewall screen. This screen allows the user to select external firewall settings for the newly created host. These are not IPTABLES[1] rules, but are instead enforced from outside of the actual host. AWS refers to a list of firewall rules as security groups. In this example a new security group is chosen, allowing port 22 (SSH) to all hosts.

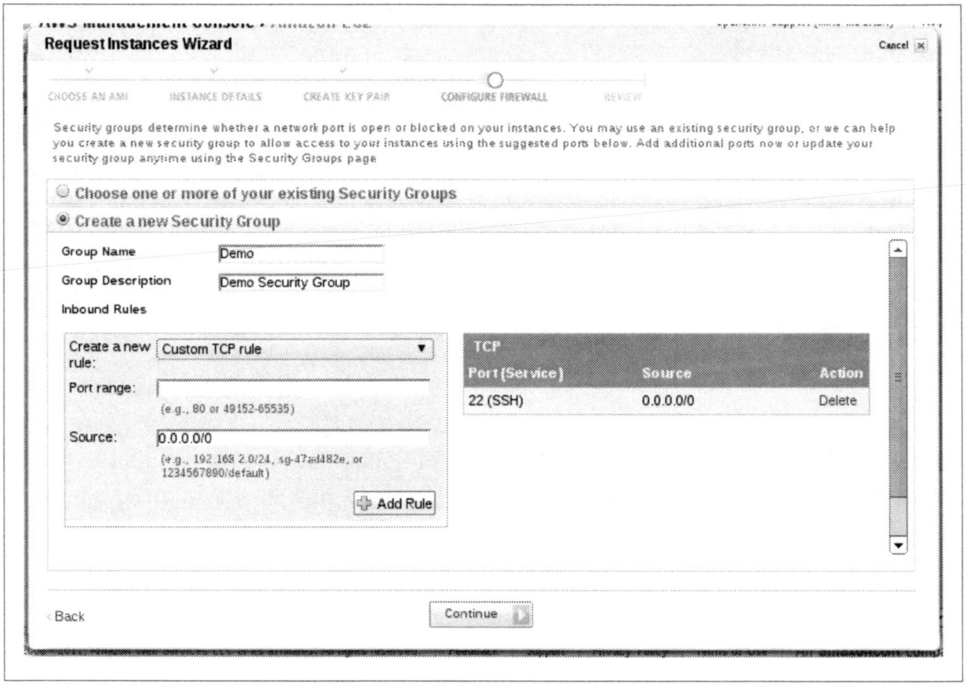

Figure 1-6. Configure Firewall

The last screen seen before launching a new instance is a simple review of all of the settings picked during the wizard. The Launch button shown in Figure 1-7 tells AWS to actually create and boot this new instance.

After launching the virtual machine, the provisioning process can be monitored on the instances page seen in Figure 1-8. In this case, it took less then a minute. Clicking on the instance reveals instance details, in particular the Public DNS entry. This is the entry point used to gain access to our newly created virtual machine.

---

1. IPTABLES is a common tool used on Linux machines to manage host based packet filtering rules

Figure 1-7. Review

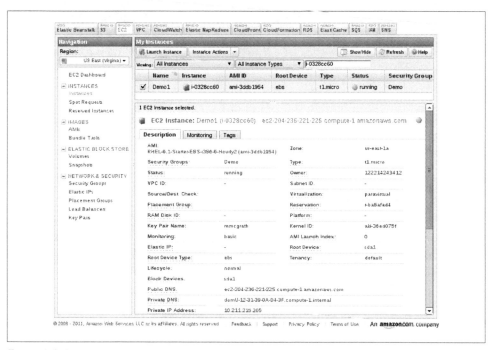

Figure 1-8. Demo1 instance page

It's highly recommended to always refer to the public DNS entry when possible. When creating custom DNS names for these hosts, try to use a CNAME. This causes requests to the host from outside of AWS to resolve to the external IP address. However, hosts internal to AWS use the internal AWS network. This private network looks like a class A (10.x.x.x) IP. All IaaS providers have some personality about things. Handy little tricks like this can be a life saver but only to those who read the docs and know them.

Using the key pair downloaded from the "Create Key Pair" step, logging in to the newly created host is easy and can be seen in Figure 1-9.

```
ec2-204-236-221-225 : root

File  Edit  View  Bookmarks  Settings  Help

[mmcgrath@desktop oreilly]$ ssh -i mmcgrath.pem root@ec2-204-236-221-225.compute-1.amazonaws.com
Last login: Fri Oct 21 21:57:56 2011 from 99.138.164.253
[root@domU-12-31-39-0A-D4-3F ~]# cat /etc/redhat-release
Red Hat Enterprise Linux Server release 6.1 (Santiago)
[root@domU-12-31-39-0A-D4-3F ~]# []




                  ec2-204-236-221-225 : root
```

Figure 1-9. SSH to new demo1 instance

Using APIs and scripts, this entire process can be automated, allowing users to create multiple instances at once. Understanding the concepts behind IaaS better illustrates how products and platforms layered on top of IaaS behave.

Platform as a Service (PaaS)

Unlike IaaS and SaaS, PaaS is a much more abstract concept. Looking at cloud computing as an entire stack, PaaS would be in the middle of that stack. With IaaS at the bottom and SaaS at the top to interface with the end users and consumers. That's not to imply all layers of the stack are required at once to consider yourself to be using cloud computing.

PaaS providers offer a platform for others to use. What is being provided is part operating system and part middleware. A proper PaaS provider takes care of everything needed to run some specific language or technology stack. Lets take a look at what it would take to provide a Python development interface and what that means for the PaaS user.

In order for Python code to be run, developers need the Python runtime and some sort of interface to expose the Python code while it's running. Some PaaS providers that support Python do it via a WSGI[2] interface. Apache, with the mod_wsgi module, is one such way to run Python applications. Developers or PaaS providers need a WSGI script somewhere so the code can be loaded and exposed via a web address.

To visualize this, think about Apache and Python at a public web address with some storage on the back end and maybe a load balancer seems pretty simple to do. Don't forget though, that there's a whole set of dependencies in order to get to that point. Apache needs some sort of operating system to function. It needs to be configured, maintained and monitored. In cloud computing, this OS runs inside virtual machines.

This gets into the details of the IaaS layer mentioned earlier. PaaS providers may do this themselves, or partner with an IaaS vendor to get it done. The important bit of information here is to know that everything from the running Apache/WSGI interface all the way down to the power and cooling in a data center, is someone else's responsibility. It is not the responsibility of the PaaS consumer.

 Many PaaS providers are providing muti-tenant solutions. This means that not only is the physical hardware shared among multiple virtual machines but the virtual machines themselves may have several different applications from several different customers on them.

PaaS today focuses almost entirely on web solutions. The components an end user interacts with are all web-based and because of this, most PaaS providers excel when it comes to large numbers of short lived process requests. PaaS providers have less polish when it comes to longer running, higher resource intensive jobs that cannot be broken down into smaller jobs. For example, a large batch processing job is likely best suited to be placed a level down at the IaaS layer because of the more fine controls over memory it provides. Scale out, not up, is becomming a common theme used throughout this book. It's not a good or bad thing, but it's a common architectural limitation. As PaaS matures, expect to see more offerings beyond web services.

---

2. WSGI stands for Web Server Gateway Interface and is a Python standard as defined in PEP 333

CHAPTER 2

Why PaaS?

Now that PaaS has been better defined and is no longer some weird cloud concept, this chapter explains how PaaS impacts different types of IT professionals. The below hypothetical example involves a fictitious, medium sized company called Widget Land, Inc. Times are tough for Widget Land partially because widget sales have been down and everyone is looking to cut costs. They're about to transform the way they do things using cloud computing and PaaS. This story starts with the most common PaaS user, a developer.

Developers

PaaS provides a care free environment for developers to work. It lets them focus on code and not have to worry about configuration and maintenance of the underlying platform. By utilizing PaaS, developers simply pick the languages and features they want, match those requirements with a provider that has them, and start coding.

Max is a developer at Widget Land. The company relies heavily on technology and has a reasonably mature IT environment. Max has an idea for a project that might completely transform Widget Land's ordering system. Max tells his boss but times are tight and they can't afford to order any new systems for this project. Max, undeterred by cost, knows this system is so efficient that Widget Land can't afford NOT to do it. Without resources, he is not sure how he can put his idea into a demo to prove to people it works. Max turns to cloud computing for the answer to his problems.

Max knows several PaaS providers have free-to-use or, at least, free-to-try offerings. He also knows he only needs a MySQL database and a JBoss provider. He spends a little time searching and finds a PaaS provider that has exactly that. He signs up and starts coding. Within a week he has something to demo to his bosses. During the demo he explains how this new system will take order processing from about 24 hours down to about 15 minutes. Everyone agrees this is a no-brainer and they tell Max to work with the rest of the team and finish the project.

System Engineers/Administrators

Cloud computing allows systems engineers and administrators to go back to doing systems work instead of server work. Over the last decade, so much of what had become a sysadmin's job is technician work, like logging in, doing updates, and replacing hard drives. It's a lot of busy work and it's often thankless. Most people don't realize the systems people are even there unless something goes wrong. Cloud computing provides a new way for admins and engineers to get back to focusing on the complicated inter-connected systems that should be their jobs.

Back to our story. James is a systems engineer who just heard about the new order processing system. Years of slow but steady growth have brought their colo to near capacity and despite several requests to find additional space, James had just been told to deal with it. Needless to say, James is worried about how he's going to find space for this new system. So James and Max sit down and go over the details of how this new code actually processes orders. The inevitable question comes up from James: "How did you get this all setup anyway? Purchases for new servers have basically been frozen for months. I know because I'm the one that normally does the purchasing."

Max gives James a quick introduction to his PaaS provider. James does the responsible thing and checks this provider out. They have a solid record on security and reliability. So James suggests maybe running it in the cloud. There will be some changes that need to be made to their own systems. They'll need the new application to securely communicate with fulfillment, shipping, and legal has some specific requirements as well. Some work to be done for sure, but no major changes.

James gets busy on setting things up in the cloud, monitoring takes less then a quarter of the time it used to. There's less to monitor because the PaaS provider is doing so much of it. Like most providers, this one has a rich API so any monitoring that is setup can easily take action on failure scenarios and automatically take corrective actions.

Later that night, James gets paged. An internal wiki for marketing and sales has gone down again. Third time this month. It's been on his fix list for a year and the hardware has been out of warranty for longer. James hates this wiki. So he has a thought, maybe this could be hosted in the cloud too? After converting, installing and locking down the new wiki in the same way the old one was locked down, James completes the conversion. Now, instead of monitoring hardware, updates, database, and so on, he just has to make sure the wiki software itself is properly maintained.

PaaS provides a unique way to provision new computing resources. APIs and web interfaces make it trivial to create new applications. This allows sysadmins to be more efficient and as long as the PaaS provider is functioning properly, there is much less responsibility.

Architects/Management

Architects like the flexibility PaaS provides. Individual computing needs, like a database, can be used without requiring internal expertise for running it. In a rapidly changing environment, this flexibility is extremely useful. Prototypes can be put together in days, not weeks or months. Technology can now be evaluated quickly and directly instead of having to rely on videos and a sales pitch.

Management likes the cost structure. No longer do projects require a large initial capital investment. These research and development costs are very tiny operating expenditures if they cost anything at all. Suddenly innovation has become the normal course of operating a business and not some special project that always seems to be on the horizon if only funds could be found.

Back to our Widget Land project. Bill, Widget Land's architect, has been paying close attention to what Max and James have been working on. One thing Bill has been tasked with this year is where to cut costs and he thinks he's found some significant savings with PaaS. Most of Widget Land's orders come in during the spring and fall over the span of a month. In the summer and winter orders always drop significantly. The current order processing system requires significant cost in computing power for those spring and fall months. Most of that hardware sits dormant in the summer and winter and even though the compute cycles go unused, they are still being paid for.

 Spiky load is great for cloud computing. In this example, increased load is seen over the span of months, but PaaS makes it just as easy to compensate for spike loads that take place over hours or even minutes.

Bill meets up with James and Max to further discuss how billing works. He's happy to see pricing models almost everywhere are usage based. Meaning they'll pay less in the summer and winter months when orders are lower. This offers significant savings over having to plan and pay for maximum capacity year round but rarely using it. After making a few changes, everything is ready to go. Max's project is a success.

Look back at this little thought experiment and it's easy to see the benefits cloud computing and specifically PaaS provided at every step of the process. The low cost R&D made it possible to plant the seed that continues to spread. Without PaaS, developer Max might not even have been able to demo this software because of a lack of resources. James, the overworked sysadmin, may not have found the capacity and time to get things integrated. Once everything was set in motion, Bill used his knowledge of his environment combined with his knowledge of PaaS to find small ways to make big cost savings.

In this example, the entire new ordering processing system was built in a public cloud via a PaaS provider. Some companies, however, are preferring a hybrid approach where many compute resources are kept private internally but when additional demand is needed, a public cloud is called upon to provide those temporary resources. This is sometimes called "Cloudbursting."

Common Features

We've discussed one basic scenario where different technology professionals all benefited in some way from PaaS. In this section, we'll dig a little deeper into what types of features PaaS providers actually offer. The first thing most people look for (and most PaaS providers advertise) is language support. There's no sense in going to a Ruby, only PaaS if what is needed is Python.

In addition to language, pay close attention to how dependencies are resolved. Some PaaS providers allow users to upload their own dependencies or automatically download what is missing. Some only allow specific libraries of specific types. Google App Engine, for example, has a knowledge base that has a list of what c modules are allowed: *http://code.google.com/appengine/kb/libraries.html*. Also listed are modules that are partially implemented as well as those that can be imported but are completely empty. This means some required libraries may not be functional at all.

Other providers, like Red Hat's OpenShift and Heroku, read through a manifest provided by the developer to automatically resolve dependencies server side. Most of this support is done using the native language tools. Ruby uses a Gemfile, Python uses setup.py and Java would use a pom.xml file. Resolution of these dependencies server side is important. Especially for non-native libraries.

specific OS and architecture versus something written in the native code of a development language. Ruby has a JSON library that helps make this distinction more clear. There's the non-native JSON library which requires a C compiler to use and link against binary libraries. There's also a Ruby native JSON library called JSON_pure written completely in Ruby.

Deciding which one to use is up to the developer. The native JSON library should run anywhere Ruby runs. The non-native C JSON may run fine on a workstation but fail when uploaded to a server if the two are not ABI[1] compliant. The native versus non-native issues go away when relying on the PaaS provider to resolve and compile these dependencies at build time.

---

1. An Application Binary Interface or ABI is used by applications to interface at a low-level with other programs or an operating system

PaaS providers often keep a local mirror or caching server for downloads. Thus downloading these dependencies should be incredibly fast.

Language selection is only one aspect of what should be considered when choosing PaaS. Another is general capabilities and feature set. Make sure to know everything an application requires before making a commitment to a specific PaaS. Since most PaaS has a free offering, this shouldn't be too hard. Most PaaS providers don't offer a lot of shared block or filesystem storage[2] options. Some offer timed jobs like cron, others do not. Almost all offer data storage of some kind either via a database or an object data store.

 Some PaaS providers offer ephemeral filesystem storage. This means it can be used but is generally not persistent and should only really be used in specific cases, like for caching.

SSL protection is another common request. Most major PaaS players offer SSL protections in at least a limited fashion.

One common thread among PaaS providers is integration with other services. Call it resale, call it partnership, call it what you want. It's a very common practice in PaaS and aligns well with cloud computing in general. The most efficient way to provide a service is to let experts run it.

Don't be afraid to get on mailing lists, IRC channels or forums. Several PaaS offerings have a rich and vibrant community. It may be a good idea to find providers that have a solid community at their core. There's no better endorsement than that of actual users in a community.

How Much Does It Cost?

Cost with all cloud computing is an interesting topic. As mentioned several times, most PaaS providers have some level of free offering. That's not to say people could run a production website on this free offering, but it is often enough to get a taste of how the service works. Spend time examining what is being charged for and what is not. Remember, not all cost comes in the form of dollars and cents. Costs can be lowered with intelligent coding. Let's look at Google App Engine.

Higher costs for CPU time, bandwidth, storage, and so on are all things to consider when budgeting. It's important to know how an application actually works before

---

2. Shared block device or file system storage is what most people are used to working with. It's common on desktops and laptops (EXT3, NTFS, and so on.

blindly hosting it in the cloud. This has always been important, but problems with an application can be amplified in the cloud. Obvious ones (memory leaks, inefficient loops, etc.) for sure only get worse when they're on a host that is sharing resources with other applications.

There are other issues to consider as well. Take an application running in Google App Engine, which currently charges for bandwidth costs. Bandwidth charges are not uncommon in the cloud. Imagine an application that requires pagination, that is simple list that only shows items 1-10, then 20-30 and so on. Now imagine a bug, that's been around forever, that has just never been noticed. This application bug caused every row in a database table to get downloaded with every page. Even though the application only displays 1-10, it's actually downloading and ignoring 11-100,000. As a result, the bandwidth sent between browser and application is very small. Just presentation and the ten rows requested. The bandwidth between the application and database is another matter

What is not being seen, but is certainly being paid for, is the requests being downloaded but not displayed to the user. This ghost traffic was never noticed before because the pages were displaying fine. By filtering 10 results at the application layer instead of the data layer the bandwidth is charging for the transfer of 99,990 results that ultimately get ignored. If this happens for every page load, there is a lot of potential savings that are wasted.

The fix? If bandwidth costs are eating up the budget, figure out how to reduce them. Only grabbing the rows needed is one way. Adding a caching layer, like memcached, is another. Most developers and sysadmins are used to doing these things for performance reasons. Considering technical fixes for cost reduction is something most IT professionals don't have a lot of experience with because it's not traditionally been a high priority in LAN environments where this type of application is typically found.

Other PaaS providers, like Heroku, have a more bulk based model. Users pay for each instance of an application. The more instances running, the higher the cost but the more theoretical throughput. Scale out, not up. Imagine your application is spread across several different machines behind a load balancer. Now imagine each of those applications is running on a host with several other applications. That's the PaaS layer at work. This concept is discussed further in the section "Computing Units" on page 32 in Chapter 5.

Add-on's, like databases, are another cost consideration. These extras are a great feature of PaaS since integration is generally automated. This is a benefit especially for proof of concepts. Comparing two nosql solutions is often incredibly easy in the cloud. Just look for providers with the right features and compare them.

Developers become more efficient in evaluations because they don't have to spend the time downloading, installing, and configuring two different technologies just to see which one to pick. These evaluations can be done in environments identical to their configuration as it would be deployed. "It ran fine on my desktop" is no longer an excuse for why things didn't work.

Development life cycle and workflow additions also increase efficiency. One such tool is Continuous Integration or CI. In a common use case, CI is basically a build system that watches over changes in a repository. Whenever an event happens (like a new tag is created or a new commit is pushed), the CI environment runs a build of that code, testing it for any errors or regressions.

This seems like a good idea on the surface but it goes much deeper then that. This workflow allows users who just committed code to get email or web based results in minutes and can fix things while the code is fresh in their mind. It functions like automated quality assurance. When using PaaS, these additions can be tightly integrated into the normal development life cycle with minimum overhead to actually operate.

Running development in the same environment as production brings about one of the most important aspects of cost in PaaS, savings. The nature of the way PaaS works leads to a great deal of efficiency when it comes to running applications, life cycle and innovation. In traditional computing it's rare to find production, staging, integration and development environments all running on identical hardware in identical setups. It's often too cost prohibitive. Virtualization helps, but only so much.

With PaaS, developers are working in the exact same environment as their sysadmins. That sort of value is hard to quantify but it lends itself to a more efficient development life cycle and fewer environmental issues discovered late in a release cycle.

Let's take another look at our phantom company, Widget Land, from Chapter 2. What would a super efficient development life cycle there look like? Remember our entrepreneurial developer Max? With CI, Max can monitor the entire team's work and run tests to confirm the new code is worthy of a release candidate. Once set up, this entire interaction takes place without Max and runs security audits, load tests, and so on. The CI then saves those results for review and can destroy any temporary PaaS applications that were created as part of the testing process. Being able to run tests in parallel against several dedicated applications takes much less time then setting up a single instance and running tests serially.

This is a perfect example of usage-based savings. Any workload that spikes up and down as a result of some requirement is ideal for cloud work. The usage-based cost model is very popular for this reason.

Maintenance

Maintenance is an ongoing, unpredictable, and often underestimated cost in computing. Doing updates, ensuring hardware is refreshed, and keeping security compliance are just some of the main subcategories of IT maintenance. PaaS greatly lowers maintenance costs due to economies of scale. This section deals with the way updates work in PaaS and where the line of responsibility lies between provider and consumer.

The first consideration is that maintenance explicitly under the responsibility of the PaaS provider and not the developer. All infrastructure maintenance falls under the PaaS providers responsibility. It would be unusual for a PaaS consumer to even know that underlying hardware is having an issue aside from outage scenarios. Additionally, most operating systems and dependent software would fall under the providers responsibility. Good PaaS providers only require the customer to maintain code they have uploaded.

What is that code exactly? This turns out to be a more complicated question than it seems. Obviously any custom written code a developer writes and uploads to a PaaS provider is their responsibility. It's possible the provider offers services like security audits, license audits or IDS[3] detection. Still, those tools only supplement regular maintenance, not replace it.

The responsibility line gets more complicated at the library layer. Some libraries are going to be provided by the platform. Others must be uploaded by the developer or specified for the platform to resolve at build time.

Generally if the PaaS provider offers a library, it's their responsibility to ensure it's functional, compatible and secure. If some library has a security vulnerability, they need to update it. Libraries provided by the developer or at build time are a more difficult

For example, Ruby developers often use gems to package and distribute libraries. If a PaaS provider does not offer a gem, like net-ldap, the developer needs to determine if the platform can resolve it at build time automatically or if they need to upload a gem as part of their code. This example Gemfile is saying not only is net-ldap required, but specifically version 0.0.3 is required.

Sample Gemfile.

```
require 'Rubygems'

# Ensure only version 0.0.3 is pulled in, nothing newere nothing older
gem 'net-ldap', '= 0.0.3'
```

In this scenario by uploading the Gemfile, a standard Ruby file, the PaaS can process the file and automatically download and compile net-ldap version 0.0.3 for the developer. This type of library resolution isn't Ruby specific and many PaaS providers sup-

---

3. Intrusion Detection Systems (IDS) assist in actively looking for security events and can take actions automatically to prevent damage.

port it. Specifying a version greater than or equal to some number is preferred so when new versions of that dependency are available, they automatically get downloaded when you next update or push your content. This is a pseudo-auto-maintained situation where effort is required from the customer to ensure deps are met and up to date, but doing so is easy.

 If a PaaS provider doesn't process dependency manifests server side, it may be possible to bundle the libraries with the uploaded code. Be careful about non-native libraries where the binaries themselves have been built and linked on a workstation that is different from the platform on the server. Non-native libraries will likely cause more pain than their worth if they're even allowed at all.

Something to be aware of with PaaS is that many providers and offerings are relatively new. Like all new things, parts of them eventually get old. Offering Python 2.6 today may seem fine but years from now it will be out of date. Pay attention to PaaS providers support lifespans and work to determine what a migration might look like.

For situations like this, it is best to work on upgrading as soon as it is feasible. Work with providers to figure out the best solution. It's likely that most if not all providers will have parallel installs of new and old offerings. For example, a PaaS might offer Python 3.0 a year before disabling Python 2.6. This is a known risk and should be properly identified when doing risk analysis. Don't just ignore it.

CHAPTER 3

What to Expect

PaaS providers often have several minor requirements in order to function properly. This means a pre-built application might not automatically work when uploaded to PaaS. Common issues are:

- Hard coded paths
- Incorrect library dirs
- Missing libraries and drivers

Many of these issues can be properly addressed in forums, knowledge bases or documentation. There should also be "hello world" type applications and examples to work from.

Remember, free offerings from providers are there for people to try it before they buy it. Production level support and features won't typically be at the free level. Additionally, features commonly relied on like scheduled jobs, memcached, databases, and so on may require additional cost from the start.

Almost all PaaS providers also have client tools of some kind. Expect to download and install them. Remember though, PaaS is supposed to make life easier.

When sitting down to write code, pay close attention to resource usage. In a PaaS environment it's important to pay attention to an individual instance footprint. Different providers call them different things, but an application cannot simply grow in memory forever on a single request. That's not how most PaaS offerings work. There are methods of doing this sort of high memory work but this isn't the *typical* use case for PaaS.

These limits vary from provider to provider. Some have soft limits which an app can grow beyond for a short time, but all have a hard limit that at some point will result in error if reached. See the section "Computing Units" on page 32 in Chapter 5 for a better description.

Some PaaS and other cloud service providers may not provide everything an application needs to function. To get around this limitation, mixing services between providers and layers may be beneficial. For example, creating an application with a PaaS but using Amazon's RDS infrastructure for the database. Just be careful about any added latency due to data center locations of the service and data store.

Notes about On-Premises PaaS

One hot topic in the PaaS world is people looking to do this for themselves. That is, install some sort of PaaS environment in-house. Turning Platform as a Service into a Platform you-do-yourself is a major undertaking. Also there aren't many options available that easily allow this today. Expect better support for these sort of products in the future.

These in-house PaaS solutions are typically more expensive as there's a higher up-front cost. The most appealing features of such a solution is customization and the sense of security that comes from running something instead of outsourcing it but requires the overhead of additional staff.

Finding the Right Provider

Spending a few Friday afternoons trying out different PaaS providers is half the fun of PaaS. It's good to get a feel for what's out there. It's important to keep a few things in mind. Look for the platform that provides the most value for a given set of problems. For example, users looking to have some soft of hosted blog software might do best to just pick a popular blog site like Live Journal. Many sites like this blur the line between PaaS and SaaS for certain, but it might have the least hassle long run.

Most of us, however, are looking to host custom written code in some language or another. Before getting there though, take a step back and think about what your application is supposed to be doing and what the requirements are.

Scale is an interesting thing to discuss and conceptualize. As mentioned before, it's important your application can scale *out* rather then *up* for PaaS. That is, do smaller operations in parallel instead of huge operations all at once. There is a more in-depth look on this topic in the section "Scale" on page 33 in Chapter 5.

PaaS providers are all working on various SLA's to ensure a high level of confidence and availability. Spend some time to determine how highly available an application needs to be. In most cases the standard SLA will work, but still spend time to get to know the SLA. Do scheduled outages count? How often will they happen? How does notification work? What about credits for unscheduled downtime beyond the SLA? These are all good questions to ask before putting an application into production.

One of the last things to look for when picking a provider is determining how their application interface works. Some providers have a proprietary code interface that tends to lock customers in to just that platform. Other platforms are open and more standardized. Spend some time to get to know an interface and determine how important it is to be able to choose a different provider later. Some users may want to host across several different platforms for added stability. Proprietary providers make this difficult and risky to do.

 Some groups, like the Cloud Security Alliance *https://cloudsecurityalliance.org/*, focus on best practices for cloud providers to use and follow. This helps give developers and other cloud customers additional assurances when committing to a cloud computing solution.

Development Workflow

Development workflow in the cloud isn't that different from traditional workflow except that it typically happens more quickly. The traditional model might look like this:

1. Write code.
2. Test code.
3. Commit code.
4. Push code.
5. QA test.
6. Declare/Tag release.

From there it might get put into a build or sent on to release engineering to be put into production. With cloud computing, tooling and testing stacks can all be used with this workflow quickly and cheaply. Continuous integration, unit tests, builds, and just about anything imaginable in a development environment can be easily automated on remote servers so there's little requirement on local compute power.

 PaaS makes it so easy to run code remotely that options are now available to do all development in the cloud. Entire IDE's exist using just a browser. All code, all everything is stored remotely.

In most cases, current development workflow can be easily replicated in a PaaS environment. Developers not wanting to use fancy bells and whistles don't have to use them, but always be aware of the options available from PaaS.

Automated Testing

Automated testing is a great way to increase reliability of code and find bugs before they reach end users. No PaaS service will write unit tests for you but some offer ways to integrate testing as part of a deployment process. Red Hat's OpenShift and

Cloudbees, for example, both offer continuous integration. Repositories can be setup to test code on every commit. This happens server side so developers don't have to give up their workstation to run those tests. Also, proper notifications and event handlers can be configured on success and failure scenarios to communicate with the entire team.

In addition to unit testing, functional testing can be done in pre-production environments. PaaS makes it much easier to script the creation of dedicated environments for testing. Functional tests can be done in an environment that is nearly identical to production. Once created, testing can be done to find performance and other issues. It's best practice to do these tests regularly and PaaS makes it easier then ever to do them.

CHAPTER 4

Examples

The examples in this chapter are designed to put some context around the previous chapters. The examples are all given using Red Hat's OpenShift platform, but those interested in other platforms can think of these as thought experiments. The general process and concepts apply to most PaaS providers and half the fun of PaaS is trying out different options and picking the best one for the job.

Create Sample Application

Everyone starts at the hello world stage. With OpenShift, it's as simple as a single command to create a publicly accessible web application. This example uses the OpenShift client tools. Many PaaS providers offer command line tools and a well documented API to allow use via existing tools. This make it easy to create and destroy entire environments via a script. As with most offerings there is also a web interface.

Installing the OpenShift client tools is easy but requires users to have Rubygems installed as well as git. Users can also use the Java client tools or eclipse plugins.

Example 4-1. Install OpenShift Client Tools

```
$ gem install rhc
```

The rest of this example assumes users have already signed up for a free account at *http://openshift.redhat.com/*. After that, users need to create a unique namespace to work in under the rhcloud.com domain.

Example 4-2. Creating DNS namespace - example1.rhcloud.com

```
$ rhc-create-domain -n example1 -l login@example.com
Generating OpenShift ssh key to /home/example/.ssh/libra_id_rsa
Generating public/private rsa key pair.
Enter passphrase (empty for no passphrase):
Enter same passphrase again:
Your identification has been saved in /home/example/.ssh/libra_id_rsa.
Your public key has been saved in /home/example/.ssh/libra_id_rsa.pub.
The key fingerprint is:
```

```
e8:4d:58:73:5e:55:89:78:69:86:e3:c6:cc:13:f9:2e example@myworkstation
The key's randomart image is:
+--[ RSA 2048]----+
|           + +.o|
|          * B . |
|       o * O    |
|       + + O .  |
|       o S o o  |
|       . o   E .|
|         . .   .|
|               |
|               |
+-----------------+
Contacting https://openshift.redhat.com/
Creation successful

You may now create an application.  Please make note of your local config file
in /home//.openshift/express.conf which has been created and populated for you.
```

This step does two things, first it registers the new DNS name *example1*. Next it sets up SSH pubkey authentication. When using git later to push code, this ssh key will be used. All applications created with this account will be $SOMETHING-example1.rhcloud.com.

Next use the tools to create a new PHP application.

Example 4-3. Create a PHP-5.3 application - myapp

```
$ rhc-create-app -a myapp -t php-5.3
Password:

Found a bug? Post to the forum and we'll get right on it.
    IRC: #openshift on freenode
    Forums: https://www.redhat.com/openshift/forums

Attempting to create remote application space: myapp
Contacting https://openshift.redhat.com/
API version:    1.1.1
Broker version: 1.1.1

RESULT:
Successfully created application: myapp

Checking ~/.ssh/config
Contacting https://openshift.redhat.com/
Found rhcloud.com in ~/.ssh/config... No need to adjust
Now your new domain name is being propagated worldwide (this might take a minute)...
Pulling new repo down
Warning: Permanently added 'myapp-example1.rhcloud.com' (RSA) to the list of known hosts.
Confirming application myapp is available
  Attempt # 1

Success!  Your application is now published here:

      http://myapp-example1.rhcloud.com/
```

The remote repository is located here:

```
ssh://0234aa0a02f24a9da313e27983731c89@myapp-example1.rhcloud.com/~/git/myapp.git/
```

```
To make changes to your application, commit to myapp/.
Then run 'git push' to update your OpenShift space
```

This command, which takes roughly 15-20 seconds to complete, creates a public application and clones a git repository. The repository is now located on the users workstation in their current working path under ./myapp/ and the actual application can be seen in a browser via *http://myapp-example1.rhcloud.com/*. The sample application is just a basic hello world application.

Making a simple change to the application involves editing the file, committing to git and then issuing a push. By doing a push, the local code changes are copied or "pushed" to the remote repo and then deployed automatically. This example adds a simple phpinfo to the end of our index.php file.

Example 4-4. Making a simple change.

```
$ cd myapp/php
$ ls
health_check.php   index.php
$ echo '<?php phpinfo(); ?>' >> index.php
$ git commit -a -m "Added phpinfo to end of index"
[master bf7edf1] Added phpinfo to end of index
 1 files changed, 1 insertions(+), 1 deletions(-)
$ git push
Counting objects: 7, done.
Delta compression using up to 4 threads.
Compressing objects: 100% (4/4), done.
Writing objects: 100% (4/4), 401 bytes, done.
Total 4 (delta 2), reused 0 (delta 0)
remote: Stopping application...
remote: Waiting for stop to finish
remote: Done
remote: Running .openshift/action_hooks/build
remote: Starting application...
remote: Done
To ssh://0234aa0a02f24a9da313e27983731c89@myapp-example1.rhcloud.com/~/git/myapp.git/
   ddf2b85..bf7edf1  master -> master
```

To summarize: this example has three elements. First, alter the landing page for *http://myapp-example1.rhcloud.com* which is an index.php file. Second, commit that change. Third push the change to the PaaS provider using git which automatically publishes.

In its most basic form, this simplicity is the power of PaaS. The examples above show the basic workflow of many PaaS providers. Create an application or compute power on some remote server. Link that remote application to development source code. Then publish changes.

More Advanced Example (Drupal)

Deploying Drupal in OpenShift.   Creating a more advanced example in OpenShift can be done via a pre-populated Drupal repository. This particular example can be found at github: *https://github.com/openshift/drupal-example*. There are four steps to take in order to download, configure and deploy Drupal.

The first step is to create a PHP application much like we did in the first example. In addition to PHP, a MySQL database will be added.

Example 4-5. Create application and database for Drupal

```
$ rhc-create-app -a drupal -t php-5.3
Password:

Found a bug? Post to the forum and we'll get right on it.
    IRC: #openshift on freenode
    Forums: https://www.redhat.com/openshift/forums

Attempting to create remote application space: drupal
Contacting https://openshift.redhat.com
API version:    1.1.1
Broker version: 1.1.1

RESULT:
Successfully created application: drupal

Checking ~/.ssh/config
Contacting https://openshift.redhat.com
Found rhcloud.com in ~/.ssh/config... No need to adjust
Now your new domain name is being propagated worldwide (this might take a minute)...
Pulling new repo down
Confirming application drupal is available
  Attempt # 1

Success!  Your application is now published here:

      http://drupal-example1.rhcloud.com/

The remote repository is located here:

    ssh://0d7e452672394ef38856c2ba264c2045@drupal-example1.rhcloud.com/~/git/drupal.git/

To make changes to your application, commit to drupal/.
Then run 'git push' to update your OpenShift space

$ rhc-ctl-app -a drupal -e add-mysql-5.1
Password:
Contacting https://openshift.redhat.com
Contacting https://openshift.redhat.com
API version:    1.1.1
Broker version: 1.1.1

RESULT:
```

```
Mysql 5.1 database added.  Please make note of these credentials:

   Root User: admin
   Root Password: M9_b8mEUdgVK
   Database Name: drupal

Connection URL: mysql://127.1.40.1:3306/
```

From this point on, the "drupal" application has MySQL access. The only thing left is to actually put Drupal in the repo (to replace the hello world app) and push it. To do this, we use git to add an upstream repo so we can keep things in sync if updates come out.

Example 4-6. Pull and push Drupal source code.

```
 # This directory was created when we ran rhc-create-app -a drupal
$ cd drupal
$ git remote add upstream -m master git://github.com/openshift/drupal-example.git
$ git pull -s recursive -X theirs upstream master
$ git push
Counting objects: 1135, done.
Delta compression using up to 8 threads.
Compressing objects: 100% (990/990), done.
Writing objects: 100% (1127/1127), 2.90 MiB | 563 KiB/s, done.
Total 1127 (delta 121), reused 1122 (delta 120)
remote: Stopping application...
remote: Waiting for stop to finish
remote: Done
remote: Running .openshift/action_hooks/build
remote:
remote: Database schema not found, importing 'drupal.sql' schema.
remote:
remote:
remote: done.
remote: ==================================================
remote:    Drupal-Admin login: admin
remote:    Drupal-Admin password: OpenShiftAdmin
remote:    Don't forget to change your drupal admin password!
remote: ==================================================
remote: mode of `/var/lib/libra/0d7e452672394ef38856c2ba264c2045/drupal/repo//php/sites/
default/settings.php' changed to 0440 (r--r-----)
remote: mode of `/var/lib/libra/0d7e452672394ef38856c2ba264c2045/drupal/repo//php/sites/
default/default.settings.php' changed to 0440 (r--r-----)
remote: Starting application...
remote: Done
To ssh://0d7e452672394ef38856c2ba264c2045@drupal-example1.rhcloud.com/~/git/drupal.git/
   0f9bf26..04ceafb  master -> master
```

That's it. Drupal is now up and running at *http://drupal-example1.rhcloud.com/*. We can confirm this via the command line using wget or a browser:

Example 4-7. Wget to Test Drupal

```
$ wget -qO- http://drupal-mcgrath.rhcloud.com/ | grep '<title>'
  <title>Welcome to OpenShift Drupal | OpenShift Drupal</title>
```

As it turns out, not many changes were required for Drupal to run in OpenShift. Mostly there was a .openshift/action_hooks/build script that needed to import the Drupal database. Then in the Drupal configs, instead of storing the database user-name and password in the repo, environment variables were provided by OpenShift and used. For those that know Drupal, this is in the sites/default/settings.php file:

Example 4-8. sites/default/settings.php

```
$databases = array (
  'default' =>
  array (
    'default' =>
    array (
      'database' => 'drupal',
      'username' => $_ENV['OPENSHIFT_DB_USERNAME'],
      'password' => $_ENV['OPENSHIFT_DB_PASSWORD'],
      'host' => $_ENV['OPENSHIFT_DB_HOST'],
      'port' => $_ENV['OPENSHIFT_DB_PORT'],
      'driver' => 'mysql',
      'prefix' => '',
    ),
  ),
);
```

Example Summary

These two examples are fairly rudimentary, but demonstrate how simple it is to get things up and running in a PaaS environment like OpenShift. In the second example, Drupal required a database which was provided and configured by the platform. Additionally, access to the database was provided via an automated mechanism (in this case environment variables). What's not demonstrated in these examples is what is required of maintenance.

In the Drupal example, some libraries were provided by the platform. By committing and pushing the Drupal code via a git repo, the user must maintain that code when updates to Drupal come out. As discussed in Chapter 3, binaries and libraries provided by the platform are typically maintained by the platform. This means OpenShift will ensure Apache, PHP and several common dependencies are properly maintained. The Drupal code, however, is the customer's responsibility, which includes watching any Drupal CVE's[1] that may be published.

---

1. Common Vulnerabilities and Exposures (CVE) are a standard used for information security vulnerability assessment and disclosure. For more information see *http://cve.mitre.org/*

CHAPTER 5

Architecture

Cloud computing is a paradigm shift from traditional computing. This means dropping existing applications in the cloud without any changes won't always work. The architecture is similar but it is different enough that one needs to, at a minimum, plan the transition. Some PaaS providers make this easier than others. Using standard and open interfaces helps. This chapter describes these changes and how to go about planning for them.

Not having to manage the infrastructure layer also means there is little control over it. Firewalls are a good example here. Most PaaS providers don't offer traditional firewall configurations. Instead some may require the developer to put IP restrictions into their code or possibly via something like Apache's .htaccess files which has the ability to allow and deny from specific IP addresses. Some PaaS providers do not support this.

Networking in the cloud is an interesting topic. For general purpose computing, most users won't notice a difference. Especially if they're just sticking with PaaS providers in a default non-redundant geographic location. There are three primary concerns when dealing with networking in the cloud.

Connectivity
> Plan for failure. This is a good idea even in traditional computing but as complexity increases so will volatility.

Bandwidth
> Remember the underlying infrastructure is shared. Bandwidth may be spiky. Plan accordingly.

Latency
> The amount of time it takes for a request to send and have the response come back also varies. If working across multiple WAN links, this can be a problem.

There are ways to mitigate these issues. Design multiple data sources in different locations. Have a proper cache that is local (or near local) to each application instance. These are complex topics but it's important that architects, systems engineers and developers take the time to know the behavior of their PaaS solution. Remember, this is computer science, not computer art. Do some experiments, document baseline performance, make some graphs and track this information over time.

Computing Units

Something not unique to PaaS but more pronounced in PaaS is the concept of a simple computing unit. Heroku calls these "Dynos," Microsoft Azure calls them "Instances." Whatever they're called, these little computing units are analogous to slices of a virtual machine. Some PaaS providers use dedicated virtual machines and don't divide them at all. They are usually composed of CPU, memory, storage and network capacity.

An individual application is running inside these *jails* with a set amount of RAM, storage, CPU, network, and so on. Some providers allow applications to burst outside of their limits for short periods of time. It's important to understand how a PaaS solution works under the hood so applications can be properly designed. Imagine the following scenario.

A nightly process job currently runs in a traditional computing environment. At its peak (which last about an hour), the amount of data being tracked in memory adds up to 1 gigabyte. The task at hand is to move this job to the cloud. There are two common ways to do this. The first is by scaling up. The second and preferred way, is by scaling out.

Scaling up is the easiest. Need more memory? Add more memory. Just as in traditional computing, sometimes the answer is just throwing bigger hardware at the problem (after all, that PaaS memory maps back to some physical memory at some point). So perhaps a larger computing unit is needed. Just find a PaaS provider that allows for larger memory stores (don't be afraid to actually contact someone and ask questions). However, scaling up isn't a good long term solution. One gigabyte of memory may be enough now, but what about next year?

The more *cloud* way to do it is also the more difficult. Instead of adding bigger resources, scale out and add additional computing power. The trick is to break the data up into smaller chunks, then communicate between those chunks. Lets say the chosen PaaS platform has computing units allowing for up to 500M of RAM at a time. They allow for some bursting, but certainly running a 1G process for an hour will get noticed (and likely killed by the underlying PaaS management services). Instead, spin up multiple computing units, one of them being a master/controller unit and the others being slaves to it.

This may be a major architectural change, but it is something developers need to get used to when working in a cloud environment. Cloud excels at processing lots of small data.

Scale

Scale is a highly complex topic and getting into scale theory isn't quite in scope for this book. Instead, this section focuses on the high level views of how architects should think about designing cloud computing systems. As mentioned several times already, in cloud computing the goal is scaling out. Often referred to as scaling horizontally. Adding more computing units is what makes cloud computing work so well. Doing so dynamically is what makes cloud affordable.

Loading a single large page isn't what most people think of as scale. Scale usually means the ability for an environment to properly process millions or even billions of requests in a short period of time.

The Slashdot effect is a classic example of websites finding out the hard way that their architecture does not, in fact, scale properly. PaaS solves the "need more" problems pretty well. Many PaaS providers have auto scaling solutions that add more computing units as demand increases. Some may require a manual touch. Worst case, users have to click through or use an API to provision additional compute power.

What PaaS providers do not do, however, is correct poorly designed code. Take this simplistic example. A PaaS provider allows for local dedicated (not shared) storage. Every compute unit gets this and storing data in it is easy. Now, lets say during development the user is used to storing session data in this storage. Session data is tied to a specific user and helps identifiy information about the user like their username. This works fine in development, where the single compute unit is all that's being used. When deploying to production though, the PaaS scaling tools add more units to deal with load. Suddenly people are randomly getting logged out.

Why? For those that have seen this scenario before it's obvious and happens in traditional computing all the time. Every compute unit is unaware of the other compute units. Meaning that when a user logs in to one unit, the others are not aware he/she has already logged in because the local storage was not shared among compute units. There are lots of ways to fix this: sticky sessions, using a shared session medium like a database, and so on. The point here is that even though PaaS requires much less responsibility of the developer, it is still their responsibility to understand the underlying systems and how they work and communicate.

One mechanism some PaaS providers are using to better deal with scale is partnering with other providers. These partnerships often focus on a specialization like DNS, email, data stores, content distribution, and so on. These solutions are worth looking at, but understand that they cannot perform miracles. For example, using non-correlated nested subqueries to iterate over database data will have poor performance in any relational databases. Same is true of missing indexes.

Spend the time to research these areas, get baselines, and do experiments. It's really the only way to truly know if code properly works in an environment. Also, don't be afraid to contact these providers for support.

Assume Failure

One common adage in cloud computing circles is that all users of cloud computing should assume failure in the cloud. What does this actually mean, though? It's not meant to ward off users from consuming cloud. It's more of an architecture virtue and it's a great one that should be applied to all computing, not just cloud computing.

The idea is simple; design systems in such a way that no single point of failure exists. Cloud Computing, in particular IaaS and PaaS, gives architects far more dynamic environments to work in. This dynamic nature means constant change and that typically increases the risk of failure.

Think about ways to increase redundancy while also increasing performance. Also look at ways to build self healing systems. Entire environments can be scripted and brought online in minutes.

Netflix took these concepts to the extreme with their now famous "Chaos Monkey." The idea behind Chaos Monkey is to not just assume failure, but actively create failure. Turn Chaos Monkey on and the Netflix environment would start seeing failures. If everything is setup properly, these failures would never lead to issues that would impact the user. While most associate Chaos Monkey with the IaaS layer, it can be applied to the PaaS layer as well.

Building a Chaos Monkey should be part of any cloud development life cycle. Think through every scenario imaginable and that is controllable. At the PaaS layer we don't have the luxury of disabling a network interface or switching an IP address (at least not easily) but the concepts should still apply. What happens when a database connection is lost or hung? What happens when applications start to balloon in memory and are killed? Spend time to think about issues that apply to the application and the PaaS environment it's in. This should never be an after thought. It should be planned from the first designs of a project.

Data

The most difficult aspect of cloud computing, really most computing, is the data layer. It is common for data to be a single point of failure. The reason for this is simple and lies in the very nature of data itself. To understand, take a deeper look at how data in a computing environment actually functions. Imagine a classroom full of students writing a paper. Now imagine that same class room, all students writing a paper, but all the same paper and all on the same physical sheet of paper.

Who writes what? When? What if one student is writing a sentence in the middle right when another student starts, too? Now, flash back to our scale talk and imagine we need to scale out. Think several classrooms, all with students. But instead of every classroom having its own sheet of paper, they all have to share the one sheet of paper that was created in that first classroom

The arrival of cloud computing brought about these same challenges and amplified them. For example, the network layer is often not dedicated and can be slower with higher latency times. To solve this problem, lots of data solutions have been created over the last few years. One of the more popular is a document or object database. Unlike a relational database, these object databases are designed to store data blobs. There are several solutions available, like Amazon's S3 or MongoDB.

These *databases* are different from a relational database and users should not just assume that data stored in MySQL could be properly ported to them. The more typical use case is with new development. These systems provide proper locking mechanisms that make the classroom issues described earlier, less of an issue.

Several of the traditional data stores are available as well, such as relational databases and filesystem storage. For those looking at private clouds, Gluster is a great place to look for distributed, shared file storage. In our example earlier, with Gluster, any student would be able to write on their paper and it would show up on everyone elses paper with a minimal delay. Similar to NFS without the NFS problems and its distributed meaning, when configured properly, nodes can go up and down without suffering data loss.

Not many public PaaS providers are offering shared file system storage of any kind at the moment. Instead they are opting for object and document stores or a relational database.

Is It Secure? Am I Secure?

Many associate security with protection from attacks by hackers. However, there's so much more to security than the script kiddies and attackers. Try to think of security in a more broad sense. Anything that disrupts a users ability to use an application could be considered a security issue. One example is the classic *grandparents* and their home computer. There is sometimes an outcry from people in the technical community with deep concerns about storing their data remotely in the cloud. With the grandparent example (which is just used to illustrate a less technical user) there is a far greater security risk storing the data locally.

Some hacker might get grandma's pictures and might even destroy them, poor grandma. The bigger risk is from trying to get grandma to manage her own backups or trying to get her to setup RAID or some other mishap. The fact is, it's just far more likely if left on her own, that something will likely happen to Grandma's local data. In the cloud, however, it gets redundancy and expert level people who's job it is to watch and maintain this information.

Now, lets take that one step further. How secure is an application's data now? Think hard about the full architecture of one of your own applications. Does it have the fully dedicated team that, say, an Amazon has? Now ask this question: Does it have PCI DSS Level 1 or ISO 27001 certifications? For the vast majority of readers, the answer is no.

Especially for any smaller start-ups. Yet, Amazon has had these certifications since 2010 and continues to get more.

Security actually fits in very well with cloud computing. It's made possible by the economies of scale. The experts all get to focus on their area, making it as solid as possible under the covers. Users of cloud computing, and PaaS in particular, get so many added benefits they may never see and never fully understand. That's by design. It's not that there's a lot of magic under the covers. It's just that there's a lot of hard work going on behind the scenes. Constant monitoring, tweaking and improvement. While it won't work for all use cases, PaaS functions well and can secure a large segment of global computing.

CHAPTER 6

Summary

Readers should now have a better understanding of PaaS, how it's different and why it matters. It's not just a change for developers, it's a change for anyone that works in IT today. Organizations that properly wield PaaS can get a strong competitive advantage in the fast moving world of technology.

The developer tools make coding more efficient while significantly lowering cost and commitment to R&D projects. This makes innovation far easier to execute and makes it easier to quickly identify and kill failures.

This book was created to give people a taste of what is out there. It's not a review of any particular PaaS and many viable PaaS solutions weren't mentioned. The fact is, there's just so many of them it would be impossible to properly give attention to them all. It's an exciting time for cloud providers. Go out, try some, and see how they can make IT easier and once again, enjoyable.

About the Author

Mike McGrath is a founding member of Red Hat's OpenShift and is currently Principal Cloud Architect with over a decade of open source systems management experience. In addition to OpenShift architecture, he serves as operations manager for all of Red Hat's Platform as a Service offerings.

Get even more for your money.

Join the O'Reilly Community, and register the O'Reilly books you own. It's free, and you'll get:

- $4.99 ebook upgrade offer
- 40% upgrade offer on O'Reilly print books
- Membership discounts on books and events
- Free lifetime updates to ebooks and videos
- Multiple ebook formats, DRM FREE
- Participation in the O'Reilly community
- Newsletters
- Account management
- 100% Satisfaction Guarantee

Signing up is easy:

1. **Go to: oreilly.com/go/register**
2. **Create an O'Reilly login.**
3. **Provide your address.**
4. **Register your books.**

Note: English-language books only

To order books online:
oreilly.com/store

For questions about products or an order:
orders@oreilly.com

To sign up to get topic-specific email announcements and/or news about upcoming books, conferences, special offers, and new technologies:
elists@oreilly.com

For technical questions about book content:
booktech@oreilly.com

To submit new book proposals to our editors:
proposals@oreilly.com

O'Reilly books are available in multiple DRM-free ebook formats. For more information:
oreilly.com/ebooks

Spreading the knowledge of innovators   oreilly.com

The information you need, when and where you need it.

With Safari Books Online, you can:

Access the contents of thousands of technology and business books

- Quickly search over 7000 books and certification guides
- Download whole books or chapters in PDF format, at no extra cost, to print or read on the go
- Copy and paste code
- Save up to 35% on O'Reilly print books
- **New!** Access mobile-friendly books directly from cell phones and mobile devices

Stay up-to-date on emerging topics before the books are published

- Get on-demand access to evolving manuscripts.
- Interact directly with authors of upcoming books

Explore thousands of hours of video on technology and design topics

- Learn from expert video tutorials
- Watch and replay recorded conference sessions